A note for parents and teachers

Everyday English introduces young people learning English to some of the most important phrases used in spoken dialogue. In realistic scenes from everyday life, characters greet each other, shop, complain, ask the way, order food in a restaurant, go to the doctor, catch a bus and meet at a party among many other situations.

Everyday English works entirely in bubble dialogue so that it is immediately clear which character is speaking. Each scene is colourfully illustrated, and every sentence and action is easy to understand and relevant to modern life.

A colourful summary of the questions presented in this book is given at the end.

The **Everyday English** workbook in this series provides further practice in the use of the spoken English that has been learned in this book, placing it in lively, stimulating activities, puzzles and crosswords.

Published by Ladybird Books Ltd
80 Strand, London, WC2R 0RL
A Penguin Company

001

ISBN: 978-0-72329-424-5

Printed in China

Everyday English

words by Valerie Mendes
pictures by Gaynor Berry

How are you?

Good morning, Henry! How are you today?
I'm well, Jim! How are you and Rose?
We're well, too... Good to see you again.

Pleased to meet you!

Hello, I'm Jim Green. Sorry to keep you waiting.
Pleased to meet you, Mr. Green. I'm Peter Henderson.
Welcome to London. Can I take your coat?

Can I help you?

Good morning. Can I help you?
Yes, please. I'd like six oranges and some bananas.
Here you are... Would you like anything else?

How many? How much?

I'd like some of those small cakes, please.
How many do you want?
I'd like eight, please... How much is that?

Can you tell me the way?

Can you tell me the way to the bus station, please?
Go down this road, and turn left. You can't miss it.
Thanks for your help!

Can you tell me the time?

BUS STOP
Excuse me, can you tell me the time, please?
It's five to three. The next bus comes in five minutes.
Oh, good! Then I won't be late!

This is for you!

This red pen is for you!
Thank you... Can I have that black one too?
Yes, you can have both!

What's that?

What's that behind your back?
What, this?
Yes, that!
It's a surprise! Happy birthday!

Are you ready to order?

Are you ready to order?
Yes, please. I'd like a cheeseburger and a coffee.
Milk and sugar?

Is anything wrong?

Is anything wrong?
Yes! This coffee's cold. Can I have another one?
Of course! I'm sorry.

Where can we buy a map?

Excuse me, where can we buy a map of London?
In the bookshop next to the bank.
Thank you very much.

What time does it start?

What time does the movie start?
Seven-thirty! And it's quarter past seven now!
Let's hurry! We don't want to be late...
ENT

I'm looking for a skirt

Good morning. I'm looking for a long skirt. Do you have any in my size?
How about this one? Would you like to try it on?
Yes, thank you, I would.

These jeans are too small!

These jeans are too small!
This skirt's too long!
Oh dear... I'm so sorry...
This T-shirt's the wrong colour!

I've lost my school bag

I've lost my school bag... Have you seen it?
No I haven't! What have you done with it
I don't know... I had it yesterday.

How often do you go?

SCH
I'm going swimming again this evening.
You are lucky! How often do you go?
Two or three times a week.

What's the matter?

You look terrible, Helen. What's the matter?
I don't know, Miss Moon. I don't feel well and I feel very hot.
Oh dear! Let me take you home.

What do you think it is?

Helen doesn't feel well, doctor. What do you think it is?
My head hurts and my ears and throat hurt too.
You have a cold, Helen. Go straight home to bed.

I'm sorry I'm late

I'm sorry I'm late, Miss Moon. I've had a cold.
Hello, Helen. I hope you're feeling better.
I'm much better now, thank you.

I like it too!

Why are you wearing that hat?
Because I like it.
I like it too... I wish I had one.

How old are you?

Hello, Monica! You look pretty! How old are you now?
I'm ten... Well, I'm almost eleven.
Well, you look very grown up!

What do you do?

Hello, my name's Sylvia. I'm from Mexico.
Nice to meet you, Sylvia. I'm Robert. What do you do?
I teach Spanish at a language school.

I want to fly to London

Good morning. Can I help you?
I hope so. I want to fly to London next Tuesday.
Let me see. Yes, there's a flight at eight o'clock.

Can you take me to the airport?

an you take me to the airport, please?
Certainly. What time's your flight?
ot until eight o'clock.
Good! Then there's plenty of time!

Some useful questions
Can I help yo
How are you?
Would you like anything else?
How many do you want?
How much is that
Can you tell me the way?
Are you ready to order?